THE COOKING CANON ENTERTAINS

Lunch and Dinner Party Menus

Rev. John Eley

D1419127

BRITISH BROADCASTING CORPORATION

Dedicated to the pleasures of the table . . . and to the friends who have shared them with me.

Cover photograph taken at the Smallbone Kitchens showroom, Studio 4, 91 Wimpole Street, London

Published by the British Broadcasting Corporation 35 Marylebone High Street, London W1M 4AA

ISBN 0 563 20363 3

First published 1985
© John Eley 1985

Set in 10pt Times by August Filmsetting, Haydock and printed by Robert Hartnolls, Bodmin

Contents

Introduction

It is for me a continual joy to be able to invite people home to share a meal. Sometimes it may simply be a bite to eat around the kitchen table, or on other occasions it may be something more formal. How can you play the part of host or hostess and be free to concentrate on the cooking? There is no easy answer, but good planning and forethought are essential.

Probably the most difficult part of planning a meal is not choosing what to eat, but who is to come. There are no special recipes for ensuring that guests will get on with each other – you have to take pot luck and say a prayer. I have been to some dinners that have really gone with a swing, and to others that have been hard work, but that is the lot of life.

I try to follow a few golden rules. If at all possible you should prepare the table a few hours beforehand so that you have a settled atmosphere for the meal. Careful planning of the menu and the timetabling of the meal helps enormously, too. Try to maintain an air of quiet calm if you can. However, if you have to scream, do – but make sure it is before the guests arrive! When it comes to lunch parties, especially working lunches, they must start on time and finish promptly . . . there needs to be a *terminus a quo* and a *terminus ad quem* to any gathering!

Grace is not only a good starter but an essential way of saying thanks and remembering others who may be far away or who have dined with you in the past.

Encouraging guests to go at the end of a meal can be more of a problem but their reluctance to leave should be taken as a compliment to your success in the kitchen and your ability to entertain. The banker Frederick Warburg used to look at his clock and say, 'Is that really the time? You naughty clock, stealing my guests away from me.' The Principal at my theological college simply used to say, 'I'm going to bed,' and promptly did so!

In the end it is not what we eat or who comes to the meal that really matters. The fact is that a group of people have managed to share some time at table together doing one of the most private things that can be done in public – that is, eating. There is no finer way of breaking down barriers, of opening up new depths in people and of sharing life and that precious commodity *time* in a world full of rush than by getting together and enjoying the pleasures of the table.

I look forward to entertaining you.

A Note about Portions

In deciding the quantities for the recipes in this book, I have planned each menu to serve generously four persons. It should be possible to work out amounts for more or less than this number by multiplying up and down as necessary, without calling in the aid of the home computer! I hope that there will always be some left-overs, though, just in case I should pop up on your doorstep!

Conversion Tables

All these are approximate conversions which have either been rounded up or down. Never mix imperial and metric measures in one recipe, stick to one system or other.

Measurements

$\frac{1}{8}$ inch	3 mm
$\frac{1}{4}$	$\frac{1}{2}$ cm
$\frac{1}{2}$	1
$\frac{3}{4}$	2
1	2.5
$1\frac{1}{4}$	3
$1\frac{1}{2}$	4
$1\frac{3}{4}$	4.5
2	5
3	7.5
4	10
5	13
6	15
7	18
8	20
9	23
10	25.5
11	28
12	30

Volume

2 fl oz	55 ml
3	75
5 ($\frac{1}{4}$ pt)	150
$\frac{1}{2}$ pt	275
$\frac{3}{4}$	425
1	570
$1\frac{3}{4}$	1 litre

Weights

$\frac{1}{2}$ oz	10 g
1	25
$1\frac{1}{2}$	40
2	50
$2\frac{1}{2}$	60
3	75
4	110
$4\frac{1}{2}$	125
5	150
6	175
7	200
8	225
9	250
10	275
12	350
1 lb	450
$1\frac{1}{2}$	700
2	900
3	1 kg 350 g

A Word about Vegetables

Sadly, vegetables in this country are all too often overcooked. The only sure way to avoid this is to watch them all the time they are cooking. Never cover green vegetables with boiling water, but place in a saucepan of water filled only a quarter of the way up. Use sea salt wherever possible. I cook greens like broccoli, cabbage and sprouts for 11 minutes and no longer. Carrots, potatoes and parsnips, indeed all root crops, take a little more cooking but 20 minutes should be long enough.

It is very important to select fresh and healthy-looking vegetables. Steer clear of the greengrocer who cannot answer your simple basic questions about the varieties and age of the vegetables he is selling. Some of the large supermarket chains buy up the best produce but ruin it in the way that they handle and care for it in the shop. So you'll probably have to look around to find a reliable supplier.

Here are a few suggested recipes.

Courgettes Provençal

1 lb courgettes, sliced in ½-inch rings	1 tbsp oil
2 oz butter	1 heaped tsp herbs of Provence

In a large oven dish melt the butter and the oil. Add the herbs and allow to sizzle for a few minutes. Then add the sliced courgettes and toss them in the butter, oil and herb mixture. Pop in the top of the oven at gas mark 5, 375°F (190°C) and cook for 12 minutes. Serve immediately.

Carrots in Orange

1 lb carrots   1 cup orange juice

Cut the carrots into thin sticks, add the orange juice
and cook over a low heat in a thick saucepan. Add salt
if desired.

Marrow

1 medium-sized marrow   2 oz butter
½ pint milk   1 dsp cornflour

Trim the marrow, remove the seeds and cut into
chunks. Boil in salted water for 10 minutes. Drain off
the water and place the marrow in a buttered oven
dish. Make a simple white sauce with the butter, milk
and flour and pour this over the marrow. Sprinkle on
some freshly grated nutmeg and bake in the oven for 20
minutes at gas mark 5, 375°F (190°C).

Purée of Vegetables

A food processor is ideal for preparing vegetables this
way. Use carrots, sprouts, turnips and my favourite,
parsnips. If you do not have enough of one, a blend of
two vegetables can sometimes be very successful
(although I would always serve sprouts on their own).

1 lb any cooked   2 tbsp double cream
   vegetable   Salt and pepper
2 oz butter

Place all the ingredients in a food processor. Blend
together. You can vary the flavour by adding nutmeg.
   If you wish, make three purées of different colours
and serve attractively presented in a single dish.

New Potatoes

1 lb new potatoes
2 oz butter
1 tbsp oil

1 clove of garlic
1 medium-sized onion,
    finely chopped

Cook the potatoes in the usual way and allow to cool. Melt the butter and oil together and add the finely chopped garlic and onion. Sauté until they are soft. Cut the potatoes up into inch cubes and toss in the oil and butter mixture. Pop in the oven and bake for 30 minutes at gas mark 5, 375°F (190°C). Delicious.

Guests for Lunch

The vicarage must be one of the few places left where the privilege of throwing lunch parties during the week can still be enjoyed. Most people have a full daily programme which excludes the luxury of time to do much lunchtime entertaining. For a clergyman, though, lunchtime is quite often a good time to catch people for an hour or so as they go about their daily labours; the thought of eating a meal that they have not had to prepare themselves often seems temptation enough to bring people together whether it is a working lunch or simply a time to spend a while getting to know each other a little better.

Living and working on the job, as I do, using the vicarage as home, office and chapel, means that I am able to take a breather from the daily round and pop into the kitchen just to keep an eye on things so that when the guests arrive all will be well, and the food ready to go straight to the table. There are a few golden rules that I try to follow. Never invite more than three guests or four at the most. Make sure the meal will not send them off to sleep in the afternoon. The food must be colourful and appetising, and the taste divine – I don't often achieve all these ideals.

The following eight menus are merely suggestions. The individual dishes are, of course, interchangeable, and nearly all simply need the accompaniment of a simple salad and some home-made lemon squash.

The final menu in this section is for a Sunday lunch. This will need a little more attention on the actual day of cooking, but there should still be time to prepare vegetables and the like, and cook the joint, between breakfast and the Sunday Service, providing you have enough courage to 'leave your oven to do the cooking without your looking'. No doubt the family will delight in cooperating as well.

Let's go to the kitchen. . . .

LUNCHTIME
MENU 1

Summer Tomato Soup
Herrings with Mustard Cream Sauce
Apple Charlotte

I always like to try and use vegetables in their proper season. Summer Tomato Soup means just what it says . . . summer is the best time to make it when English tomatoes are at their most flavoursome. The first time I had this soup was with some friends by a watermill in Suffolk when it was served ice-cold from a vacuum flask. It does no harm to add a few ice-cubes.

As a child we were always able to enjoy herrings, living as we did in Suffolk, not too far from the fine fishing grounds of the North Sea. Then when these were allowed to become overfished, the only herring-bones you saw were in the weave of jackets. I have been delighted to see the advertisements declaring that 'Herrings are back', but to tell you the truth, if you knew the right people and places to look you would never have known they had gone. This is a simple dish to prepare and is delicious with fresh brown bread rolls and salad.

Queen Victoria is said to have had this recipe for Apple Charlotte served to her on the Isle of Wight. The Bramley is undoubtedly the most excellent English cooking apple. This dish can be prepared for baking the day before and enjoyed as a left-over when cold. I thank Mrs D. Langston of Warwick for bringing this version of a classic dish to my attention.

Summer Tomato Soup

2½ lb ripe red tomatoes
1 lime
A few dashes tabasco
1 oz caster sugar
Salt
½ pint double cream

8 oz cooked smoked gammon
4 large spring onions, chopped
1 diced cucumber
2 sticks diced celery
4 tbsp freshly chopped basil

Deseed and skin the tomatoes and purée them in a food processor. Add to this the tabasco and the juice of the lime. Now add the rest of the ingredients, stirring gently. The vegetables should be very fresh. Serve well chilled.

Herrings with Mustard Cream Sauce

1 herring per person
1 glass Riesling
1 dsp chopped parsley
1 small clove of garlic

1 medium-sized onion, chopped
5 fl oz soured cream
1 5-ml tsp French mustard
Salt and black pepper

Ask your fishmonger to clean and take the heads off the fish if you can't face doing it yourself. Chop the onion and garlic finely and sprinkle with the chopped parsley over the herrings, lying opened on a shallow dish. Season with salt and black pepper and pour over the wine. One glass is not usually enough, but for modesty's sake! Allow to stand in a cool place overnight.

Place the fish in a pan and pour over the marinade. Cook gently, remembering to turn the fish once, for about 12 minutes. Remove the fish on a serving dish, cover with foil and keep hot.

Gradually blend the French mustard (I usually use the Dijon *fine* variety) with the cream in a thick saucepan and heat gently, adding the stock the fish cooked in a little at a time. Bring to the boil once. Pour over the fish and serve garnished with croûtons.

Apple Charlotte

1 lb Bramley apples	3 oz butter
6 oz caster sugar	6 thick slices of bread
Spices to taste: ground cloves, nutmeg, ginger, cinnamon	1 tbsp brandy
	Cream for serving

Peel, core and slice the apples. Place in a pan with 2 oz of the butter and cook until you have a purée. Stir in the caster sugar and the spices to taste.

Butter the slices of bread on both sides and line a 1-pint basin with them. Keep one slice for the top. Fill with the apple purée, cover with the remaining slice of bread and sprinkle some more caster sugar over, with a pinch of nutmeg. Bake in an oven at gas mark 4, 350°F (180°C) for about 45 minutes.

Turn the charlotte out onto a dish and flambé with the warmed brandy. Serve with cream.

LUNCHTIME
MENU 2

Game Pâté
Salmon Pancakes
Honey Icecream

Earlier this year I was presented with an express-delivered package by the postman with the complaint, 'It smells a bit, Vicar.' The poor man had never lived in the country so he could not appreciate the aroma of hung game. Inside was a fine brace of pheasants from a kind friend. In a later recipe you will discover what I did with the breasts, but the game pâté given here will serve well as a starter or hors d'œuvre, or just as a delicious snack. It can be made in season and then frozen.

I highly recommend pancakes, with a tasty savoury filling, for a lunchtime menu. You can use all kinds of fillings, so after you've tried this one (which I first came across at 'Le Petit Châtelet' restaurant on Paris's left bank overlooking the Seine and Notre Dame) why don't you experiment with your own ideas as well?

My neighbour when I was living in the close of Carlisle Cathedral, Canon Richard Bevan, was affectionately known to us as the 'Rev Bev'. Now that I have moved away, I miss him, not only for his friendship but because he had an inexhaustible supply of rosemary, which always survived the rages of the Cumbrian winter. The same aroma welcomes me to parts of Var in Southern France when I go there on holiday. The recipe for Honey Icecream uses only natural gifts – honey, cream, eggs and rosemary. It simply is a taste from Heaven.

15

Game Pâté

12 oz dark pheasant
    meat
8 oz belly pork
6 oz smoked gammon
6 oz best minced beef
1 large onion, chopped
2 oz butter
1 beaten egg

4 oz breadcrumbs
1 large tsp herbs of
    Provence
1 large clove of garlic
2 generous measures
    Armagnac
1 large orange
Seasoning

Coarsely mince the pheasant meat, belly pork and gammon together and mix with the minced beef. Sauté the onion gently in the butter until it is soft. Crush the garlic and add to the pan. Sauté for a few minutes. Remove from the heat and stir in the breadcrumbs and beaten egg along with the herbs and seasoning. Combine thoroughly with the meat mixture and finally add the Armagnac.

Fill a 1½-pint lidded terrine with the mixture and push down well. Slice the orange and lay the four centre slices on top of the pâté. Seal on the terrine lid with a paste of flour and water, or cover with foil. Stand in a tray of hot water and bake in the oven at gas mark 3, 325°F (170°C) for about 1½ hours. Take out of the oven and allow to cool before placing in the refrigerator. You should keep it for a couple of days before serving.

Salmon Pancakes

Pancake mixture
4 oz plain or wholemeal
    flour
2 large eggs

½ pint milk
2 tbsp vegetable oil
Pinch of salt

Filling

1 6-oz tin red salmon, flaked and drained	3 tbsp soured cream
1 small chopped onion	1 beaten egg
1 tbsp chopped parsley	Grated Gruyère cheese
8 oz cooked, mashed potato	5 fl oz single cream

I usually make the pancake mixture in my food processor; or you can use a liquidiser. Sift the flour and salt together into the food processor, with the eggs. Process for a few seconds. Add the oil and then process again, gradually pouring in the milk. Pour the mixture into a jug and allow to stand for a few hours in the refrigerator.

To make the filling, mix together all the ingredients except the Gruyère cheese and the single cream. Place a tablespoon of the mixture into each pancake. Roll them up and fold in the edges, and place them on a greased baking dish. Sprinkle them with the grated cheese and the cream and bake in an oven at gas mark 2, 300°F (150°C) for 20 minutes.

Honey Icecream

6 egg yolks	1 fresh rosemary sprig
¼ pint honey	¾ pint double cream

Beat the egg yolks until they are light and fluffy. Gently heat the honey with the rosemary sprig in it until it just reaches boiling point. Retrieve the sprig and pour the honey onto the egg yolks, beating all the time. Beat in the cream and gently heat the mixture, being very careful not to let it boil. Remove from the heat and allow to cool before freezing in a plastic container.

17

LUNCHTIME
MENU 3

Cromer Crab Bake
Cheese and Potato Pie
Raspberry Syllabub

Off the Norfolk coast near Cromer, a few miles out to sea, there is a twelve-mile-long underwater shelf where the Cromer crab comes to give birth. As you drive around the coast there in the early months of summer you will see lots of signs, handwritten by local fishermen, offering delicious Cromer crabs for sale, ready cooked you will be glad to know. John Williams, who with a friend makes it possible for us to obtain these crabs almost anywhere from London to Liverpool (you may have to ask around a little), tells me that the season runs now from April to October. They are delicious just by themselves, but prepared the way suggested here they make a really delicious part of a menu, whether as a starter or a main course. Made with fresh ingredients, this can be prepared in advance and frozen.

Memories of school meals send shudders of horror mixed with childhood delight down my spine as I look back . . . oh, for that chocolate crunch . . . and oh, how we dreaded the cheese and potato pie. But now I have found the secret of success – and it is so simple that I am almost embarrassed to include it here. Use really excellent ingredients, and you cannot go wrong. You can eat this Cheese and Potato Pie as a main course, as here, or as a side vegetable with another meal.

Raspberries must surely be considered one of the fruits that can be most successfully frozen. I am amazed that some of the supermarket chains go to countries as far away as Bulgaria to find fruit for freezing. Did you know that in Scotland they grow the finest raspberries in Europe? Raspberry Syllabub always goes down well and is a delicious complement to any meal.

Cromer Crab Bake

4 dressed crabs (depending on size)	1 dsp plain flour
1 pint cooked mussels	$\frac{1}{4}$ pint milk
2 hard-boiled eggs	$\frac{1}{4}$ pint fish stock made
1 tbsp chopped fresh fennel	from white fish bones, onion, bouquet garni
1 clove of garlic	and a bay leaf
1 tsp ground ginger	4 oz breadcrumbs
1 tbsp vegetable oil	1 oz butter
	Salt and black pepper

Remove the crabmeat from the shells. Chop the cooked mussels coarsely. In a food processor blend together the eggs, fennel and garlic clove, finally adding the ginger.

Heat the oil and flour in a thick saucepan and gently add the milk to make a smooth sauce. Add the fish stock. Simmer for about 10 minutes, stirring all the time. Remove from the heat and stir in the herb mixture and finally the crabmeat and mussels. Season to taste. Place the mixture inside the crab shells or on some scallop shells. Sprinkle with breadcrumbs, dot with butter and fire under a very hot grill.

Cheese and Potato Pie

2 lb cooked mashed
  potato
8 oz cheddar cheese,
  strong flavoured
4 oz butter

2 tbsp soured cream
1 large onion, finely
  chopped
2 large eggs
Salt and pepper

Ideally the potatoes need still to be hot when you begin to make this deliciously simple lunchtime meal. Place them in a food processor or in a mixer with a large bowl. Grate in the cheddar cheese and add the butter and soured cream. Process or mix for a few seconds before adding the rest of the ingredients. The onion does need to be very finely grated or chopped before being added. Make sure that there are no lumps of potato left and that the mixture is smooth.

In the meantime butter a deep-sided ovenproof dish (I use a soufflé dish for this). Place in an oven at gas mark 5, 375°F (190°C) for about 40 minutes.

This is delicious served with a crisp green salad.

Raspberry Syllabub

8 oz raspberries
2 tbsp Cointreau
1 glass sweet white wine

2 oz caster sugar
½ pint double cream

Bruise half the raspberries with a wooden spoon and sprinkle with half the sugar and the Cointreau. Place a little of this mixture at the bottom of individual wine-glasses.

Beat the cream with the sugar until stiff and then gently add the wine, beating all the time. Finally blend in the remaining raspberries.

Spoon this mixture on top of the raspberries in the wineglasses. Chill and serve.

LUNCHTIME
MENU 4

Cream of Watercress Soup
Chicken Paella
Strawberry Icecream

It was to Mary Sumner House, the vicarage in the Winchester Diocese where Mary Sumner is said to have conceived the idea of the Mothers' Union, that I went for my interview or, as they called it, 'Selection Conference' for the Church's Ministry. I can remember being one of the last to arrive. As I walked in the room all the other candidates stood up – they had apparently thought I was one of the selectors, being bald and worn by life a little, I guess! When I took off my coat and they saw my jeans, they quickly realised their mistake. There is always time to pop out from conferences such as these and on one excursion I discovered some superb watercress beds. I longed to get home to the kitchen to try a recipe given me by dear friends of mine, Ian and Kay Hamel-Cooke, a clergyman and his wife who had opened many doors for me when I was young and intolerable! Kay is an excellent cook and this soup is delicious.

Children love bitty food, and this simple Chicken Paella is therefore a delight to them as it is full of good things they can pick out, and leave the rest – usually the rice. And it can certainly bring back memories of happy holidays in Spain. An ideal dish for the whole family as well as for guests.

Don't try this recipe for Strawberry Icecream unless you feel like making it again and again – your friends and children will never want to eat the commercial kind again. There are so many icecream makers on the market these days that it's not impossible that you know someone who has one. But even if you are unable to get hold of one, this recipe is so easy and oh, so good. If I want to be really extravagant I sometimes sneak a little strawberry liqueur into it!

Cream of Watercress Soup

2 bunches of watercress	$\frac{1}{4}$ pint single cream
6 spring onions	1 oz flour
2 oz butter	Salt and pepper
$\frac{3}{4}$ pint chicken stock	1 lemon
$\frac{1}{4}$ pint milk	

Finely chop the onions and sauté them in 1 oz butter along with some salt and pepper. Do not burn the onions! Finely chop the watercress, stalks and all, and add this to the onion in the pan and again sauté lightly. Add the chicken stock and cook for about 15 minutes. In another pan melt the rest of the butter with the flour and cook for about a minute before adding the milk. Remove from the heat and allow to cool for a few minutes before adding the single cream. Grate in the rind of the lemon and squeeze the lemon juice into the watercress. Add the two mixtures together and blend in the liquidiser or food processor. Adjust the seasoning and heat. Serve with crisp white bread.

Chicken Paella

5 tbsp cooking oil	1 clove of garlic
1 lb raw chicken meat	$1\frac{1}{2}$ pints chicken stock
8 oz gammon	1 thimbleful saffron
1 large onion, chopped	2 level tsp salt

1 lb easy-cook long grain rice	1 large green pepper, sliced
4 oz frozen peas	1 lemon
1 15-oz tin tomatoes	12 green stuffed olives
4 oz peeled prawns	1 pint mussels
Black pepper to taste	

In a heavy casserole heat the oil and then slice the chicken into strips and fry gently until it is cooked. Add the gammon to the pan along with the chopped onion. Continue to fry gently for 10 minutes. Add the tomatoes, stir in the chopped garlic, stock and saffron and bring to the boil. Add the salt and pepper and stir in the long grain rice, peas and prawns. Finally arrange the green pepper on the top and seal down the lid well with foil and then cook in the oven at gas mark 4, 350°F (180°C) for 45 minutes. Have a look after 30 minutes just to make sure all is well. Taste and check seasoning, and when it is cooked decorate with lemon, stuffed olives and mussels.

Strawberry Icecream

| 8 oz strawberries | 1 pint double cream |
| 6 oz icing sugar | |

Blend all the ingredients together and freeze for 40 minutes in a metal tray. Stir with a wooden or silver spoon, and freeze again.

Even if you do not have an icecream maker, you cannot go wrong with this recipe. It is out of this world.

LUNCHTIME
MENU 5

Tuna Fish Mousse
Chicken Pie
Sarah's Mango Chill

Although often scorned, tinned tuna fish makes a tasty contribution to a meal. This recipe for Tuna Fish Mousse was sent to me by a friend from Dorset, Ruth Stocker.

One Sunday we had rather more chicken left over than we knew what to do with. By Wednesday we still had not exhausted the left-overs and so I launched forth into the kitchen and threw a few things in a pot and made a sauce; and so was born this Chicken Pie recipe. It freezes superbly.

One of the joys of being a parish priest is the opportunity it gives to make new friends. That joy is even greater when one of them passes on a new recipe. Sarah Craig gave me this one for Mango Chill. It gives me great pleasure to reproduce it here so that others can enjoy it.

Tuna Fish Mousse

1 8-oz tin tuna fish	3 tbsp water
½ pint milk	½ oz gelatine
1 bay leaf	3 tbsp double cream
¾ oz butter	2 oz prawns or shrimps
¾ oz flour	1 egg white, whipped
¼ pint mayonnaise	Watercress for garnish

Heat the milk with the bay leaf in it; work the butter and flour together, and blend with the milk to make a sauce. Allow to cool. Pound or process the tuna fish until it is very smooth and fold into the sauce, along with the mayonnaise and lightly whipped cream. Dissolve the gelatine in the water and add to the sauce, mixing well. Coarsely chop the prawns and add them to the mixture. Finally fold in the beaten egg white.

Lightly oil a mould and pour the mixture in. Leave to set in a cool place, covered, ideally in a refrigerator.

Turn the mould out onto a serving dish and garnish with watercress.

Chicken Pie

1½ lb chopped cooked chicken meat	1 medium-sized can of sweetcorn, or ½ lb frozen sweetcorn
1 large onion, finely chopped	3 tbsp red pepper, chopped
1 oz butter	3 tbsp green pepper, chopped
1 tbsp plain flour	4 tbsp celery, chopped
½ pint milk	8 oz button mushrooms
½ pint stock or water	Salt and black pepper

Pastry

12 oz SR flour	3 tbsp water
1 tsp mixed herbs	6 oz butter or margarine
Pinch of salt	1 egg

To make the pastry, sift the flour, salt and herbs into a bowl. Beat the egg and the water together. Rub the butter into the flour, and gradually add the beaten egg and water until you have a good dough. (You can make the pastry in a food processor. Simply add the flour, salt and herbs to the bowl and blend for a few seconds. Chop the butter up a little and add it; blend again until you have a crumbly mixture. Finally, gently pour in the egg and water until the dough forms a ball.) Leave the pastry to cool in the refrigerator for a few minutes before using.

Carefully pick all the meat off the chicken bones, discarding the skin. Gently fry the chopped onion in the butter until it is soft, then add the stock or water and the plain flour. Gradually pour in the milk and, if necessary, a little more water. Make a fairly thick sauce and season it well with the salt and pepper. Add the meat and the rest of the ingredients, and gently stir together for a few seconds.

Line a large pie dish with the pastry, making sure you have left enough for a lid. Allow the mixture to cool for a while before putting into the pastry. Seal on the lid with a little egg yolk and glaze the top. Bake in the oven for 45 minutes at gas mark 5, 375°F (190°C).

Sarah's Mango Chill

2 large mangoes
4 egg yolks
4 oz caster sugar

A few drops of vanilla
   essence
1 pint milk
$\frac{1}{4}$ pint double cream

Choose two ripe mangoes (they should look as though they have died in the swamps!). Peel them and mash or blend to a smooth purée.

Blend together the egg yolks, the sugar and the vanilla essence, and gently pour in the milk. Place on a low heat and continue to stir until the custard thickens. Allow to cool for about an hour and then blend in the mango purée and the double cream.

Pour into glasses and chill.

This is a surprisingly delicious sweet . . . you will be sure to want to try it again.

LUNCHTIME
MENU 6

Asparagus Soup
Fréjus Tuna Fish
Burnt Sunrise

The Vale of Evesham and a good deal of neighbouring Worcestershire, where I am living now, are famous for fresh vegetables and the good things of the garden, so I am lucky in the spring to be able to buy some of the most delicious and tender asparagus that is available. It may seem a sin to turn it into soup, but once you have tasted it I am sure you will feel that it was worth it.

There is a very fine Roman arena at Fréjus in the south of France which, with typical French ingenuity, they have turned into one of the finest outdoor stadiums in Europe for pop concerts and the like. This Fréjus Tuna Fish dish is so named because some friends I met down there on holiday gave it to me as a supper dish. I think the Hastings family would agree with me that it's just the thing for an easy and very tasty meal.

Japan, the Land of the Rising Sun, is the inspiration for Burnt Sunrise. With the advent of their melon liqueur, we have turned something very simple into something very special.

Asparagus Soup

1½ lb fresh asparagus
1 pint chicken stock
2 oz butter

2 oz flour
1 egg yolk
5 fl oz single cream

Salt and pepper
Freshly grated nutmeg

Chopped parsley for
garnish

Cut the washed asparagus into 1-inch strips. Simmer in half the stock for about 15 minutes. Remove from the heat, add the rest of the stock and simmer again for about 20 minutes. Liquidise or process this mixture until it is smooth. Melt the butter in another pan along with the flour and make a roux sauce with a little of the purée. Cook for about 2 minutes. Add the cream with the egg yolk and grated nutmeg; then add the rest of the purée and season. Heat through gently and serve. Garnish with the chopped parsley.

Fréjus Tuna Fish

12 oz tuna fish, canned
$\frac{1}{4}$ lb mushrooms, chopped
1 green pepper, chopped
1 red pepper, chopped
2 tbsp Bran Flakes
1 tsp dried mint
1 15-oz tin chicken soup

1 15-oz tin chopped tomatoes
1 chicken stock cube
6 oz grated cheese
8 oz pasta shells
1 oz butter
Salt and black pepper
A dash Worcestershire sauce

Drain the juices off the tuna fish and flake into a casserole. Throw in the rest of the ingredients except the pasta shells, grated cheese and butter, and mix gently. Cover and cook in a slow oven, gas mark 4, 350°F (180°C), for about an hour. In the meantime cook the pasta shells, drain and toss in the butter. When the casserole has cooked stir in the pasta shells and sprinkle the grated cheese on top. Pop in the oven at a high temperature for about 10 minutes.

Be prepared for them to come back for more – make double the quantity just in case!

Burnt Sunrise

1 lb dried apricots	2 egg yolks
1 measure melon liqueur	6 oz demerara sugar
$\frac{1}{2}$ pint double cream	

Soak the apricots overnight, then simmer gently for 30 minutes. Place in a shallow dish and pour on the measure of melon liqueur.

Beat together the cream and the egg yolks and pour over the mixture. Scatter the demerara sugar on top and brown under a red-hot grill.

LUNCHTIME
MENU 7

Seafood Salad
Summer Pork and Spiced Apricots
Pineapple Poll

One thing is certain – we certainly do not make enough of the wealth of seafood found around our coasts. Last summer I met a man walking up the steep path from Lulworth Cove in Dorset carrying a large spider crab and struggling with his diving gear. When I tried to engage him in conversation I discovered he was German – I think! – but he did manage to indicate that the unfortunate crustacean was to be his lunch. Would an Englishman eat a spider crab? On the other side of the country, at Wells-next-the-Sea in Norfolk, the fishermen still boil their whelks in special sheds by the shore before taking them to the processing factory where they are blast frozen to be sold in 2-kilo packs. The addition of a few cockles to the Seafood Salad I offer here improves it no end.

The Summer Pork with Spiced Apricots is very easy to prepare. I would suggest that you cut the slices thinly as pork is such a rich meat. This can be beautifully dressed and presented to make a superb centrepiece to a cold buffet.

Pineapple Poll is great fun to make but it needs to be done at the last minute. For this reason I would hesitate to give it at a dinner party as by the time you have reached the sweet course you probably won't feel much like cooking! But try it for a special lunch. It takes courage . . . skill . . . and flair – as well as a very hot oven!

Seafood Salad

6 oz peeled and cooked
  prawns
2 oz cooked cockles
1 large red apple
4 oz walnut halves

5 fl oz soured cream
1 dsp French Dijon
  mustard
Juice of 1 lemon
1 dsp tarragon vinegar

A deliciously simple starter this one, or an interesting addition to a salad menu. Thaw the prawns and cockles if using frozen ones. Wash and cut the apple up into small cubes and toss in the lemon juice. Blend the mustard, vinegar and soured cream together in a large bowl and add the rest of the ingredients, folding them in gently. Chill well before serving.

Summer Pork and Spiced Apricots

3 lb loin of pork
3 tbsp clover honey
1 tbsp wine vinegar

1 tbsp made English
  mustard
Salt
Vegetable oil

For the Spiced Apricots
1 lb dried apricots
3 tbsp wine vinegar
Cinnamon stick

6 cloves
6 oz demerara sugar
½ pint water

Add the apricots to a saucepan with the spices, sugar and vinegar and ½ pint of water. Gently simmer until cooked and leave to cool overnight.

Ask your butcher to bone the meat, and reserve the bones for a stock (you can always freeze them and use them later). Score the rind of the pork and rub all over with salt and oil to make a nice crackling. Place in a roasting pan.

Set the oven at gas mark 5, 375°F (190°C). Put the joint in the middle of the oven and allow to cook for 1½ hours, then increase the temperature to gas mark 7, 425°F (220°C). Blend the honey, mustard and vinegar together for the glaze. Remove the joint; spread the mixture over it, and replace in the oven to cook for a further 30 minutes.

Allow to cool overnight and carve in thin slices. Serve with the spiced apricots.

Pineapple Poll

2 large pineapples	4 oz caster sugar
4 egg whites	

Sorbet

1 lb fresh raspberries	$\frac{1}{4}$ pint water
$\frac{1}{2}$ lb redcurrants	4 oz sugar
1 lemon	

Prepare the sorbet by making a light syrup with the sugar and water and the juice of one lemon. Wash the fruits and purée in your food processor. Add them to the syrup. Turn into a plastic dish and freeze for 40 minutes. Take out, beat with a wooden spoon or silver fork, and freeze again.

Meanwhile, slice the pineapples in two and remove the woody core. Scoop out the juicy flesh and dice it. When the sorbet is ready, fill each pineapple shell with a good portion. Cover with the pineapple chunks, and then make a meringue mixture by beating the egg whites until really stiff and folding in the caster sugar.

Have the oven ready at its hottest temperature. Cover the pineapple with mounds of meringue and pop in the oven for 6 minutes. The waiting is agony! Serve immediately.

LUNCHTIME
MENU 8

Grapefruit and Grape Salad
Sunday Special Leg of Lamb
The Nutty Parson's Folly

Sunday lunch is probably one of the most enjoyable meals of any week. The Grapefruit and Grape Salad is the inspiration of Ruth Graysbrook, a friend of long standing. I think you will find it is most refreshing, even after the driest of sermons!

Lamb is a very special treat that I always enjoy. The only problem, though, is that butchers these days seem to be in such a rush to get it on the market. So if you want to serve it at its best, make sure you keep it for a few days in the refrigerator or chill room. I think you'll find that the combination of flavours in this dish really does enhance the taste of the meat, and also makes a delicious gravy.

There's a tradition at the vicarage that the youngest person at the table has the first serving of pudding, and then we work backwards through the ages after that. You should see the children's faces when they realise that they get the choicest portions . . . perhaps the Parson is nutty!

Grapefruit and Grape Salad

3 large grapefruit
6 oz Muscat grapes
2 oz chopped almonds

1 tsp chopped fresh mint
1 tsp caster sugar
French dressing

Peel the grapefruit and cut out the segments. You will need to be sure-fingered and have a really sharp knife for this. Make sure you discard as much of the pith and the skin between segments as you can. It is advisable to do this over a bowl to catch the juice.

Peel the grapes by popping them in boiling water. The skins will then come away easily. Cut out the pips with a very sharp knife.

Place the grapefruit segments mixed with the grapes in individual serving glasses. Sprinkle over the chopped almonds and caster sugar. Chop the fresh mint finely and sprinkle that on top. Finally, trickle over a little French dressing. Cover with film and chill well before serving.

Sunday Special Leg of Lamb

3–4 lb leg of lamb	1 lb smoked back bacon
1 large onion	6 sprigs rosemary
2 large carrots	$\frac{1}{2}$ lb apricot jam
2 heads chicory	$\frac{1}{2}$ pint chicken stock
3 sticks celery	Salt and black pepper
1 oz butter	
2 tbsp oil	

Cut up all the vegetables. Heat the butter and oil together, add the vegetables and fry gently for a while. Place in the bottom of a roasting dish. Take the leg of lamb and make six deep incisions in it, cutting right down to the bone. Into each incision push a rasher of bacon and a generous sprig of rosemary. Place the rest of the bacon rashers over the lamb to cover it. Melt the apricot jam gently in a saucepan and ladle it over the joint until it is well covered. Place the joint on top of the vegetables, and then pour the stock over the vegetables, adding lots of black pepper and salt.

Cook in the oven at gas mark 5, 375°F (190°C), allowing 25 minutes to the pound and 25 minutes over.

When you lift the joint out of the oven you will see that the jam has gone black. Don't panic . . . that is what is meant to happen. Place the joint on a serving dish and keep warm. Strain off the juices into a pan and thicken with a little cornflour if liked. Remove the blackened bacon from the joint and arrange the vegetables around it. Serve with the delicious gravy.

The Nutty Parson's Folly

8 oz ginger biscuits, well crushed	Pinch of salt
6 oz butter	1 tbsp water

Filling

1 lemon	2 oz caster sugar
4 oz hazelnuts	5 fl oz double cream
2 eggs	

Topping

1 lb fresh or frozen raspberries	1 tbsp arrowroot
	1 large measure gin

Melt the butter gently and blend in the biscuit crumbs, salt and water. Press the crumb mixture into an 8-inch flan tin and allow the base to cool in a refrigerator.

For the filling, finely grate the rind of the lemon and squeeze the juice. Finely chop the hazelnuts. Mix all the ingredients together, whisk for 2 minutes until creamy, and then pour onto the biscuit-crumb base. Bake in an oven at gas mark 4, 350°F (180°C) for 15 to 20 minutes. Allow to cool.

Drain the juice from the raspberries if frozen, and add to it $\frac{1}{4}$ pint of water. Blend this with the arrowroot and gently bring to the boil for 1 minute. Remove from the heat and stir in the gin. Place a layer of raspberries over the cream filling in the tin, and spoon the sauce over.

Dinner Party Menus

We move now from lunchtime parties to those evening occasions when we are enabled to indulge in a little luxury and good food. What a difference a well-prepared table, a few flowers and candles make to a room. I always like to have a lighted candle on the table at home to remind us of absent friends. I think the tradition is originally a Danish one.

Cooking for a dinner party can be very demanding, and yet the person who does all the work in the kitchen somehow has to appear cool, calm and collected and ready to act as host once the guests start to arrive. I still remember one of the very first dinner parties I ever gave. It was for a girlfriend, and at the time I was working in London and living in a small bedsit in Sloane Gardens. The kitchen was actually the top of a lift shaft, one of those service lifts that used to bring the dishes up from 'below stairs'. The first course had gone off well, but just as I was going to collect the main course there was an earth-shattering crash. I opened the lift door to find that what had been my kitchen was now in a thousand pieces on the ground below . . . we ended our meal in a Lyons Corner House.

I hope nothing like that ever happens to you. My chief piece of advice is that you plan your dinner party well beforehand, giving careful thought not only to who comes but to what you have to eat. In the following menus I offer a few suggestions. Like the lunchtime menus, the dishes are all interchangeable. I hope you will enjoy them.

Salmon Lime Jelly
Louise's Summer Chicken
The Admirable Pie

The American palate seems to be able to cope extremely well with weird and wonderful mixtures of things sweet and savoury. I remember an extraordinary breakfast once enjoyed by an American hitch-hiker we picked up in the Lake District one summer. We gave him a bed for the night and next morning we found him sitting down to his typically English breakfast – spreading strawberry jam on his fried bread! I have tried Salmon Lime Jelly on some American friends and I'm glad to say they were delighted with the result.

Louise had been to America with her parents, and had taken pleasure in collecting the menu cards from the various 'diners' they ate out in. Louise's Summer Chicken is the result of purloining not only the menu card, but the recipe itself from the chef. It is delicious, and easy to do.

The Admirable Pie is made to be admired and enjoyed. It is rich and tempting, and will appeal to anyone with a sweet tooth. Be warned – a little goes a long way.

Salmon Lime Jelly

6 oz tinned salmon	1 lime
1 pint-sized pkt lime jelly	1 tsp mint sauce
1 pint water	

Dissolve the packet jelly in the scant pint of water. Add the juice and finely grated rind of the lime. Stir in a teaspoonful of mint sauce. Allow to stand and cool for a while.

Place a little tinned salmon in the base of individual ramekins (allow about 1 oz per serving) and pour some of the jelly over to fill the ramekins. Allow to cool, and then place in the refrigerator and chill well.

Allow the left-over jelly mixture to set and then chop it up. To serve, turn the ramekins out onto chilled plates and pile the chopped-up jelly around them. Decorate each helping with a sprig of mint.

Louise's Summer Chicken

2½–3 lb chicken breasts	1 oz plain flour
1 large onion	½ lb mushrooms
2 eating apples	½ pint chicken stock
2 tbsp butter	8 fl oz double cream
½ tsp paprika	Salt and black pepper
2–3 tsp curry powder	

Melt the butter in a thick saucepan and add the chopped onion and apple. Cook gently for about a minute before adding the curry powder and the paprika. Stir in the flour gradually and cook for another minute before adding the stock, and finally the sliced mushrooms. When the sauce has thickened a little, add the cream off the heat.

Butter a shallow ovenproof dish and lay the chicken joints in it, skin upwards. Season with salt and black pepper. Pour over the sauce and bake in a moderate oven, gas mark 4, 350°F (180°C), for about 1½ hours. Do not cover.

The Admirable Pie

2 limes
8 oz ground almonds
8 oz caster sugar
8 eggs, separated
1½ pints double cream

4 oz candied cherries
1 tbsp orange-flower
  water
1 oz icing sugar
2 oz butter

Butter a 9-inch cake tin. Finely grate the rind of one lime into a bowl and add the ground almonds, 4 oz caster sugar and two egg whites. Mix together thoroughly and spread into the buttered cake tin. Bake in a slow oven, gas mark 1, 275°F (140°C), for about 20 minutes. Remove.

Peel the limes, remove the seeds and cut into quarters. Place in a thick saucepan and cook gently for a few minutes before adding the rest of the sugar and the cream over a very gentle heat. Stir in the egg yolks one by one until the mixture begins to thicken. Allow to cool for a few minutes before spreading over the ground-almond base in the cake tin.

Chop the candied cherries and spread them over this mixture. Take the rest of the egg whites and whisk them until stiff with the orange-flower water. Spread on top of the cherries and sprinkle with the icing sugar.

Bake in the oven at gas mark 2, 300°F (150°C) for 15 minutes or until the meringue is done.

Trout Pâté
Pork 'Slosh'
Friar's Omelette

This recipe for Trout Pâté was supplied to me by a lady whose husband keeps a trout farm in Cumbria, not far from Penrith. As well as brown trout, they also breed the very large pink trout that are delicious cooked as steaks (or can be used in this recipe as well). I once asked them if they had problems with herons going after their fish. The answer surprised me. They had more trouble with the goats jumping in after them!

I think when you read the recipe the name Pork 'Slosh' will explain itself. It is a surprisingly quick way to cook pork, and very good too. As a variation, add half a wineglass of lemon juice to give another nuance to the flavour.

People are always sending me cookbooks, and I am very grateful for them too. Friar's Omelette comes from a very old and battered book with no cover so I don't know who wrote it, but it makes a delightful end to a meal.

Trout Pâté

1 lb cooked trout (see method)	3 fl oz double cream
Juice of 1 lemon	1 clove garlic
4 oz cottage cheese	Freshly grated nutmeg
3 fl oz mayonnaise	Salt and black pepper

There are two ways of preparing this delicately flavoured dish. There's the 'all in one' method – 'I haven't got a minute to spare, so let's pop it all in the food processor'. Or there's the 'They're coming to dinner next weekend . . . I've got bags of time' method. I must confess that I usually have to go for the first one. However, let's look at the second, supposing you have the time.

Gently poach the trout in a little milk until you can simply pull out the back fin. Skin the fish and discard the bones. Allow the flesh to cool, sprinkle with lemon juice, cover and leave to stand in a cool place overnight. Blend together the rest of the ingredients and chill, covered, overnight. In the morning mix the two together. For a coarse pâté do it with a fork; if you require a more refined one, use a food processor. Serve chilled with brown bread and butter.

Pork 'Slosh'

1 lb pork fillet, cubed	Salt and white pepper
½ oz butter	5 fl oz double cream
1 medium-sized onion, finely chopped	'Slosh' of dry white wine
¼ lb mushrooms, sliced thinly	

In a thick casserole melt the butter and gently fry the onions until they are opaque. Then add the sliced mushrooms and fry for a further minute. Add the cubes of pork fillet (they need to be fairly small) and sauté until slightly browned. Season with salt and white pepper. Add the double cream and cook fairly quickly until the cream thickens. Add a good 'slosh', or if you prefer 'slurp', of dry white wine. Turn down the heat and cook fairly slowly for about 20 minutes.

Friar's Omelette

1 lb Bramley apples
4 oz caster sugar
2 eggs, well beaten
2 oz butter
1 lemon

2 tbsp milk
8 oz digestive biscuit
   crumbs
1 tbsp cold water

Peel, core and slice the apples and put in a saucepan with the water and the sugar. Stew until they are cooked. Stir in the butter, milk, grated rind and juice of one lemon and the eggs.

Butter a shallow, round pie dish and spread half the biscuit crumbs over the bottom. Add the apple mixture, spread the rest of the biscuit crumbs on the top, and bake in the oven at gas mark 5, 375°F (190°C) for 30 minutes.

Turn out and serve.

DINNER PARTY
MENU 3

Smoked Haddock Chowder
Savoury Pork Slice
Chocolate Ginger Trifle

Vera Stewart's Smoked Haddock Chowder has to be commended. She very kindly introduced me to it at a dinner party just as I was about to leave Carlisle, and for that gift I am very grateful. It pays to make a largish quantity as it freezes well. In place of the dry sherry I have also used Vermouth to good effect.

Savoury Pork Slice provides a contrast to the starter. Full of good things, it goes down very well at a dinner party and is also an ideal dish for a buffet or cold luncheon.

I can't remember where I found this recipe for Chocolate Ginger Trifle. It is very rich, very naughty and very delicious . . . and I love it.

Smoked Haddock Chowder

1 lb smoked haddock
   fillet
2 pints chicken stock
1 bay leaf
1 pinch mace
1 onion, chopped
2 sticks celery, chopped
2 oz butter
1 tsp curry powder

1 oz flour
1 tbsp oatmeal
3 potatoes
$\frac{1}{2}$ pint milk
$\frac{1}{4}$ pint soured cream
2 tbsp dry sherry
2 tbsp chopped parsley
Salt and black pepper

Gently poach the haddock fillets in a large saucepan with the stock, bay leaf, mace and a little pepper. Bring to the boil and simmer for 5 minutes. Remove the fish and set it aside. In another saucepan melt the butter and add the onion, celery, curry powder and flour. Cook for 2 to 3 minutes. Remove from the heat and allow the sizzling to stop. Pour on the fish stock, return to the heat and bring to the boil, whisking all the time. Sprinkle on the oatmeal and simmer for 10 minutes.

Dice the potatoes and boil for 6 to 8 minutes until they are tender. Strain, add the milk and cream and season before heating through again. Stir in the sherry and serve hot, sprinkled with fresh parsley.

Savoury Pork Slice

Meat Loaf Mixture

1½ lb pork sausage meat
1 oz butter
1 small onion, chopped
1 tsp dried sage
3 tomatoes, skinned and
    chopped

4 oz breadcrumbs
1 tbsp parsley
1 large egg, beaten
2 large slices cooked
    ham (optional)

Stuffing

1 small onion, chopped
4 oz cooking apples,
    chopped
2 oz raisins

1½ oz breadcrumbs
1 oz toasted almonds
1 tsp thyme
1 oz butter

8 oz puff pastry

Egg to glaze

Make the stuffing first. Lightly cook the onion and the apple together in the butter. Add the rest of the ingredients, and bind together with an egg or a little milk if necessary. Leave to stand for a while in a cool place.

For the meat loaf, fry the onion gently in the butter. Mix all the other ingredients together in a bowl and then add the onion, and bind all together. Grease a 2-lb loaf tin and sprinkle some breadcrumbs on the inside. Place half the meat mixture in the loaf tin. Add the stuffing in a layer, and then the rest of the meat. Press down firmly and bake in an oven at gas mark 4, 350°F (180°C) for about 1¼ hours.

When it is cooked, turn the meat loaf out to cool. Wrap the slices of ham around the loaf, if used, and cover with a case of puff pastry. Brush well with beaten egg and a little salt and bake for about 30 minutes at gas mark 7, 425°F (220°C) until it is golden brown.

This is delicious served with pickled walnuts.

Chocolate Ginger Trifle

1 lb ginger cake
¼ pint ginger wine
1 tbsp honey
2 tbsp chopped stem
   ginger
1 2-oz pkt chocolate
   buttons
1 tbsp caster sugar

2 egg yolks
1½ tbsp cornflour
1 pint milk
6 oz plain chocolate
10 fl oz double cream

Place the sliced ginger cake in the bottom of a serving dish. Heat the ginger wine and the honey together and then pour over the cake. Chop up the stem ginger and the chocolate buttons and sprinkle on top.

Whisk the egg yolks and the caster sugar together with the cornflour. Place in a thick saucepan and gently add the milk before bringing almost to the boil. Grate the chocolate and add this to the mixture. Stir until it thickens. Cook for a little while longer, remove from the heat and stir in half the cream. Pour this mixture over the sponge. Allow to chill. Decorate with whipped cream, candied cherries and angelica.

DINNER PARTY
MENU 4

Potted Shrimps
Pork Chops with Apple and Raisin Sauce
Cumberland Rum Nicky

If you can get hold of Morecambe Bay shrimps, they are delicious in this Potted Shrimp recipe (another example of the superb seafood that is found off our shores). Once again, I must thank Ruth Graysbrook, whose cottage in Sherborne has been the scene of many a fine meal, for this.

It's always difficult to know what to do to prevent grilled pork chops becoming dry. The apple and raisin sauce offered here solves the problem with a fine combination of flavours. Another recipe for a quick sauce requires simply 2 tablespoons of honey and 1 of wine vinegar heated together in a saucepan and then poured over the cooked chops – delicious.

We return to Cumbria for a tasty pudding. Margaret Lamb, a home economist at Newton Rigg Agricultural College, is very keen on traditional Cumbrian recipes and this Cumberland Rum Nicky is one of them. We've often judged cookery competitions together, and recently our choice of winner was vindicated when the person we'd selected went on to win a national competition.

Potted Shrimps

12 oz cooked and peeled
  shrimps
6 oz butter

Pinch of mace
Salt and pepper
6 oz chopped walnuts

Melt the butter gently in a thick saucepan over a low heat and season with the salt, pepper and mace. Add the shrimps and stir gently over the heat for about 6 minutes, coating each one well with the butter.

Remove from the heat and add the chopped walnuts. Gently pack the shrimps with their butter into small ramekins. Cover with film or extra butter after they have cooled, and place in a refrigerator.

Heat gently in their ramekins in a low oven to serve. Sprinkle some parsley on the top and squeeze on some lemon juice, and offer hot buttered toast with them.

Pork Chops with Apple and Raisin Sauce

1 pork chop per person
2 cooking apples
2 oz butter
4 tbsp redcurrant jelly
2 dsp cider vinegar

2 tsp Worcestershire
  sauce
2 oz raisins
A dash tabasco

Trim the fat from the chops and grill gently, or better still barbecue in the open air!

Peel, core and slice the apples and fry them gently in the butter. Add the redcurrant jelly, cider vinegar, and the other ingredients and bring to the boil. Simmer for about 5 minutes.

Remove the chops from the grill and place on a serving dish. Pour over the sauce. Serve with buttered potatoes and a green salad.

Cumberland Rum Nicky

4 oz chopped dates
1 oz stem ginger
2 oz butter
1 oz soft brown sugar

2 tbsp rum
Egg white to glaze
½ tbsp caster sugar

Pastry
6 oz plain flour
Pinch of salt
4 oz butter

1 tbsp caster sugar
1 egg yolk
A little water

Make the pastry by sifting the flour and salt together. Rub in the butter. Add the caster sugar and the egg yolk, and a little water, if necessary, to mix and bind. Knead lightly and form into a ball. Leave wrapped in the refrigerator for a while.

Now for the filling. Chop the dates and the ginger. Cream the butter and sugar together and add the rum and beat well.

Line an 8-inch flan tin with two-thirds of the pastry. Sprinkle the chopped dates and ginger over the base and spread the rum butter mixture on top. Use the rest of the pastry to make a plaited or lattice-work top. Brush with a little egg white and sprinkle with caster sugar. Bake in a moderate oven, gas mark 5, 375°F (190°C), for 30 to 45 minutes.

Serve just warm. I don't really think that you will want cream with it, but if desperate you had better have a little to hand!

Redcurrant Savoury Jelly combines sweet and sour flavours, but if you prefer to use aspic mixed with redcurrant jelly preserve, instead of a packet jelly, it will be less sweet.

The blend of fish and mushrooms in Sole Stuffed with Shrimps and Mushrooms is a traditional one, all the better if you can get hold of some chanterelle mushrooms. They are usually sold dried in this country. Some people make the mistake of overcooking the fish so that it toughens – don't forget that, if kept covered, a little cooking goes on after the dish has been removed from the oven.

My earliest acquaintance with chestnuts was not an altogether happy one. My brother and I, with a friend, had gone to a copse near our home on the farm in Suffolk to find some fresh ones. Unfortunately, it was a very hot day and we managed to disturb a wasps' nest . . . I never knew I could run so fast! Since then I have found it safer to buy chestnut purée in tins, now so widely available. This Chestnut Chocolate Pudding is very good.

Redcurrant Savoury Jelly

1 pkt raspberry jelly
1 pint water
2 tbsp redcurrant jelly
  preserve
1 orange

6 or 8 oz coarsely
  minced left-over lamb
Twists of orange rind to
  garnish

Dissolve the packet jelly in the scant pint of water. Add the juice and the finely grated rind of the orange. Allow to stand until cool.

Place a little of the meat (about 1 oz per helping) in the bottom of individual ramekins and spoon on a little redcurrant jelly. Pour over the dissolved jelly to fill the ramekins and allow to cool before placing in the refrigerator.

Allow any of the jelly mixture that is left over to set. To serve, turn the ramekins out onto chilled serving plates. Chop up the reserved jelly and spoon it around the base. Garnish each helping with a piece of twisted orange rind.

Sole Stuffed with Shrimps and Mushrooms

2 fillets of sole per
  person
1 glass dry white wine
$\frac{3}{4}$ pint water
1 medium onion, sliced
Bouquet garni
6 oz shrimps, cooked
  and peeled

8 oz button mushrooms
4 oz butter
4 level tbsp plain flour
2 limes
Salt and pepper
Parsley

Be sure to ask your fishmonger for the trimmings from the filleted fish. Place with the bones in a pan with the wine, water, onion, bouquet garni and the grated rind of the limes (reserve the juice). Cover the pan and simmer for about 30 minutes. Strain off the stock.

Divide the shrimps between the eight fillets of sole and roll them up. Place in an ovenproof dish. Pour on the stock until it is halfway up. Cover the dish with foil and cook in an oven at gas mark 4, 350°F (180°C) for about 15 minutes until the fish is tender.

In the meantime, slice the mushrooms and sauté with 2 oz butter. Remove the fish from the oven and drain off liquor. Cover and keep warm. Melt the other 2 oz butter in a thick pan and stir in the flour, making sure to cook it for 1 minute. Slowly stir in the stock and bring to the boil. Simmer for 3 minutes.

Drain the mushrooms and spoon them over the fish. Season the sauce with salt and pepper and finally add the lime juice. Pour over the fish and garnish with chopped parsley.

Chestnut Chocolate Pudding

1 15-oz tin unsweetened chestnut purée	8 oz Bourneville chocolate
5 oz caster sugar	A generous measure rum
5 oz unsalted butter	Cream to decorate

Melt the chocolate in a basin over a small pan containing a little boiling water. Blend together the caster sugar, butter, chestnut purée and rum. When the chocolate has cooled a little add to the mixture.

Place in a serving dish and chill for several hours. You can pop it in the freezer if you are in a hurry, but be sure to bring it out about an hour before serving.

Decorate with cream and serve.

DINNER PARTY
MENU 6

Venison Pâté
Chicken and Dolcelatte Roulades
Chestnut Icecream

Sometimes the simplest things are the best, and this Venison Pâté is one of them. It can be used also as a delicious sandwich filling. Venison is widely available now in a variety of cuts, so this is well worth a try.

Contrasting flavours that you discover by surprise can often delight the palate. The fine Italian cheese Dolcelatte is still comparatively unknown in this country. I know very little about its history but adore its taste, and I hope you will enjoy the contrasts of flavours in this simple dish as much as I do.

At Radio Cumbria I was responsible for a cookery slot every Saturday morning. Sometimes I would wake up in the middle of Friday night in a cold sweat realising that I had not thought out the dish for the following day. This icecream recipe proved to be very popular despite the fact it was a moment of midnight inspiration.

Venison Pâté

1 lb venison trimmings	Pinch of coriander
¼ pint stock	Salt and pepper
1 clove	2 oz butter
Pinch of thyme	1 glass port
Pinch of mace	

Mix all the ingredients, except the butter and the port, and place in a lidded earthenware casserole. Seal on the lid with foil or a paste. Bake in a moderate oven for 2½ hours until very tender.

Remove from the casserole and place in a food processor or a liquidiser. Add about 2 oz butter and a generous glass of port and mix to a good consistency.

Place in an earthenware dish and pour over some melted butter. Allow to chill well for a couple of days.

Serve with hot buttered toast.

Chicken and Dolcelatte Roulades

8 oz Dolcelatte cheese	1 glass good red wine
4 oz pistachio nuts, chopped	¼ pint chicken stock
4 chicken breasts	Salt and black pepper
8 rashers smoked streaky bacon	1 level tsp arrowroot
1 tbsp vegetable oil	1 lemon
1 oz butter	

Allow the cheese to stand for about an hour after bringing it out of the refrigerator. Finely chop the pistachio nuts and blend them together with the cheese into a paste. Place the chicken breasts between two sheets of greaseproof paper and beat them flat with a rolling pin or meat hammer. Spread the cheese mixture evenly over the four chicken breasts and roll them up. Wrap two pieces of bacon around each piece of chicken and secure with a cocktail stick.

In a thick casserole gently melt the butter and oil and brown each 'parcel' of chicken well. Add the salt and pepper. Add the red wine and stock and bring to the boil. Cover and gently simmer for about 35 minutes. Remember to turn each 'parcel' from time to time. When the chicken is cooked remove from the pan and

53

keep in a warm place. The arrowroot needs to be blended with a little water until it is smooth, then pour into the pan juices, add the juice of the lemon and stir until it thickens. Spoon the sauce over the 'parcels' and serve.

Chestnut Icecream

1 15-oz tin unsweetened natural chestnut purée	4 oz caster sugar
¾ pint double cream	1 miniature of rum, or a few drops of rum essence
4 eggs	

Separate the eggs and beat the egg yolks well with the caster sugar and the rum. Stir this into the chestnut purée and mix well for about 3 minutes. Allow to stand. Whisk the double cream until it is thick and the egg whites until they peak and then fold into the purée mixture. Stir well, preferably with a wooden spoon. Place in a plastic mould and freeze.

Before serving remove from the freezer for about 30 minutes and allow to stand at room temperature.

If you have time, make some meringue cases and place a portion of icecream in the middle of each. Pour over some chocolate sauce.

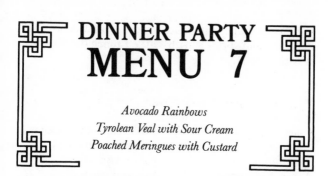

Avocado Rainbows
Tyrolean Veal with Sour Cream
Poached Meringues with Custard

A simple and refreshing starter to the palate are these Avocado Rainbows. Make sure you use a very sharp paring knife to prepare the citrus fruit so that you remove all the tough and tasteless pith. It is really best to cut your avocado with a silver-plated knife if possible, too.

It is a little unsual to use rosé wine in cooking, but the effect with this Tyrolean Veal is very pleasing. This fairly rich dish is always well received.

The Poached Meringues with Custard is really a dish from nursery days and is often known in this country as Floating Islands. However there is also a belief that it has its roots in the Burgundy region of France. Served chilled and sprinkled with a little Praline, it will delight adults as well.

Avocado Rainbows

½ a large avocado pear	1 large orange
per person	French dressing
1 pink grapefruit	

Cut each avocado in two and place on a serving plate, one half per person. Peel and segment the orange and the grapefruit.

Over the half avocado make a 'rainbow effect' with

55

the slice of grapefruit, a slice of orange, and so on. Chill very well and sprinkle with a little French dressing just before serving.

Tyrolean Veal with Sour Cream

1 veal escalope per person	2 tbsp capers in vinegar
2 oz butter	5 tbsp soured cream
2 tbsp plain flour	½ pint rosé wine
1 small onion, chopped	Salt and pepper

Take two sheets of greaseproof paper and a rolling pin. Place the escalopes of veal between the paper and bash them well all over so that they double in area. This is a very satisfying therapy for the frustrated cook! Season about half the flour with salt and pepper and coat the veal escalopes with it. Melt half the butter in a frying pan and gently fry the escalopes for about 5 minutes on each side until tender and golden. Remove and keep the escalopes covered and warm. Sauté the chopped onion.

Melt the rest of the butter in the pan and add the remaining flour; cook for a minute or so. Add the capers in their vinegar and the rosé wine and cook until the sauce thickens. Stir in the soured cream, add the veal to the pan and heat through gently. Serve with plain boiled rice or small new potatoes. Deliciously quick and simple.

Poached Meringues with Custard

4 eggs	2 tbsp water
5 oz caster sugar	1 vanilla pod
1 pint milk	

In a large saucepan put the milk, water and vanilla pod and heat until it is just below boiling. Separate the eggs and beat the whites, adding 3 oz sugar, until they are really stiff. With two spoons gently make large egg shapes with the meringue mixture and poach each one in the milk for 2 minutes per side. Remove them, and allow to drain on a large dish.

Remove the vanilla pod from the milk. Beat the egg yolks and the remaining sugar together, and then add a little milk from the pan. Now add this mixture to the pan with the milk. Stir over a low heat until the custard thickens. Pour into a shallow serving dish and float the meringues on the top.

Chill well before serving.

DINNER PARTY
MENU 8

Smoked Mackerel Pâté
Beef with Stout and Prunes
John Peel's Grave

I was about to give a small cookery demonstration for the Mothers' Union in a church just outside the Close in Carlisle, but first of all I had to go to sing evensong. I put some boil-in-the-bag mackerel fillets on the stove and went off to church. Halfway through the service I suddenly remembered the pan still boiling on the ring. It was the fifteenth evening, and the Psalms go on for ever on the fifteenth evening . . . I was the only clergyman present! Service over, and the minor canon was seen, robes flowing, running apace back to the house to find a pall of black smoke filling it. Have you ever smelt boil-in-the-bag mackerel flavoured with melted plastic? Not a gastronomic experience! The addition of a little tot of whisky to the pâté does help, but do try to avoid the plastic bag.

Beef with Stout and Prunes is one of those casseroles that is ideal for a late summer evening dinner party. It is especially good made with Guinness.

Caldbeck in Cumbria is where John Peel is buried, and the recipe for the jam used in this pudding was given me over his grave by Mrs Satterthwaite who spotted me looking around the churchyard while she was on her way to a neighbour with a jar of it. I must say it makes a super base to a steamed pudding. This recipe is a little tongue in cheek, but well worth a try if you have a glut of rhubarb.

Smoked Mackerel Pâté

12 oz smoked mackerel
¼ pint soured cream
4 oz butter
4 oz cottage cheese
1 lemon
3 tbsp horseradish sauce
Salt and black pepper
1 measure whisky

Skin the mackerel, and remove the bones. Place all the ingredients in a blender or food processor and mix until the pâté has reached the required consistency.

Fill a stoneware dish and chill well before serving with hot buttered toast.

Beef with Stout and Prunes

3 lb good-quality stewing
    steak
2 tbsp plain flour
½ tsp mixed herbs
3 tbsp cooking oil
½ lb sliced onions
½ lb sliced carrots
2 bay leaves
½ pint stout
8–10 large prunes
Salt and black pepper

Soak the prunes overnight in the stout. Season the flour with the salt, pepper and mixed herbs. Cut the meat into good-sized chunks and coat them well with the seasoned flour.

Heat the oil in a thick casserole and brown the meat well on all sides. Remove; add the sliced onions and gently cook them until they are tender. Add any residue of flour, return to the meat to the casserole and add the rest of the ingredients except the prunes. Place the casserole with a well-sealed lid in the oven and cook for about 3 hours at gas mark 2, 300°F (150°C). During the last half-hour add the prunes.

John Peel's Grave

For the jam
1½ lb dried figs
2 lb rhubarb

4 oz plain flour
4 oz butter
4 oz caster sugar
2 eggs

4 lb sugar

Grated rind of 1 lemon
½ tsp baking powder
2 tbsp milk

Cut the rhubarb up into 2-inch pieces, mix in the dried figs and add the sugar. Leave to stand overnight and then bring gradually to the boil and cook for about 15 minutes, stirring regularly. Saucer test for setting, as for any jam.

Spoon 6 tablespoons of the mixture into the bottom of a 1½-pint pudding basin. (You can pour the rest into 1-lb jam jars and preserve.)

Mix the flour and baking powder. Whisk together the butter and sugar until it is light and fluffy. Beat in the eggs separately and lightly stir in the flour and lemon rind, along with the milk. Pour into the basin, cover with foil and steam for 1½ hours.

You can of course use any other jam, but this one is fun because of the story associated with it.

DINNER PARTY
MENU 9

Herring and Bacon Rolls
Rabbit in Piquant Sauce
Russian Pie

This herring dish provides an interesting start to a meal. Do try it – herrings and bacon seem to be made for each other.

Rabbit in Piquant Sauce is an old recipe which I first enjoyed in the South of France when we had to stay at a hotel after the car broke down. It was a gastronomic delight. It does seem a pity that we don't make as good use of game as the French do.

The recipe for Russian Pie was given to me by L. John Holman after I had done a book-signing session in Gloucester. He tells me that his mother used to make it around Christmas time as an alternative to the traditional pudding. This is the first Russian dish I have tried.

Herring and Bacon Rolls

1 small herring per person
2 slices smoked streaky bacon per person
1 shallot
1 oz butter
2 oz oatmeal
1 large egg, beaten
Salt and black pepper

Ask your fishmonger to fillet the herrings for you. Make sure that he descales them as well. Roll each herring fillet up with two pieces of bacon, baste with the beaten egg seasoned with a little salt, and then roll in the oatmeal.

Melt the butter in a thick saucepan and season with salt and pepper. Finely chop the shallot and sauté for a while until soft. Transfer to a cooking dish and place the rolled fillets on top. Baste with a little more butter and bake in an oven at gas mark 5, 375°F (190°C) for about 15 minutes.

Serve with brown bread and butter.

Rabbit in Piquant Sauce

4 lb rabbit joints	1 tsp thyme
1½ tsp ground ginger	2 bay leaves, crushed
Salt and black pepper	8 fl oz chicken stock
2 tbsp vegetable oil	½ tsp cayenne pepper
8 oz small onions	(optional)
1 Bramley cooking apple	4 fl oz soured cream
1 clove of garlic	

Season the rabbit joints with salt, pepper and ginger. Heat the vegetable oil in a large heavy pan and cook the rabbit for about 10 minutes until it is well browned all over. Remove to a plate. Add the onions to the oil and stir them over a high flame until they are well browned. Add the apple by grating it into the pan. Add the garlic, thyme and bay leaves whilst stirring. Return the rabbit pieces to the pan and pour over the stock. Add the cayenne pepper if required. Cover and simmer over a low heat for about 40 minutes. Just before serving place the rabbit joints on a warmed ovenproof dish, stir the soured cream into the sauce and pour over.

Russian Pie

3 large oranges
2 lemons
4 eating apples
2 eating pears
6 oz demerara sugar

4 oz currants
4 oz sultanas
4 oz raisins
½ tsp cinnamon

Pastry
12 oz SR flour
Pinch of salt
2 oz caster sugar
6 oz butter

Finely grated rind of 1
    orange
2 eggs

Make the pastry by mixing together the flour, salt and sugar. Rub in the butter and then the grated rind of one orange. Gently mix in the eggs to make a dough. Place the pastry in a plastic bag in the refrigerator.

Now peel the oranges and the lemons for the filling, making sure as much as possible of the pith is removed. Slice them with a sharp knife and place them in a saucepan. Core the apples and pears and cut into eight. Fold in the sugar and the rest of the ingredients and cook gently for 20 minutes. Take off the heat and allow to cool for a good while.

Grease a 10-inch shallow cake tin with a little butter and line with the pastry, leaving ⅓ for the lid. When the fruit mixture has cooled, pack it into the pastry mould. Roll out the lid, place on top and seal with a little milk or beaten egg. Paint the lid with egg glaze and a little caster sugar and bake in the oven for 35 minutes at gas mark 5, 375°F (190°C).

Delicious with cream.

Flamiche of Leeks, Bacon,
Mussels and Cream
Fillet of Lamb Orange
Strawberry Marquise

A Flamiche is a Belgian pastry dish. This tasty recipe was given me during a cookery demonstration by a chef in Cumbria, part of a special dinner party at which I was honoured to be a guest. The pastry case is made from puff pastry – I must confess that I often use the frozen variety rather than make my own because it is so much easier.

Fillet of lamb is now widely available at many supermarkets and is a succulent and delightful discovery. Orange and lamb go well together and, because of the cut, there is little fat. Fresh rosemary is best in this recipe, but the dried kind will do.

We stay with the tastes of summer to sample Strawberry Marquise, a recipe sent me by Kathleen Dyson from Sherborne. You do not have to be a professional cook to make a great hit with this. The flavours are enhanced by the Kirsch – if only it was not so expensive!

Flamiche of Leeks, Bacon, Mussels and Cream

8 oz frozen puff pastry	6 oz cooked mussels
6 oz smoked bacon	8 fl oz double cream
1 oz butter	1 egg
1 large leek	Salt and pepper

Dice the bacon and sauté it in the butter. Add the finely chopped leek and soften it, seasoning with a little salt and pepper. Add the double cream and allow to thicken a little. Last of all, add the mussels and allow to cool.

Roll out the puff pastry and cut out eight equal-sized rounds 4 inches across. Damp the sides of the pastry with beaten egg and place a tablespoon of the filling mixture in the centre of four of the pastry rounds.

Seal on a lid and knock back the edges with a knife. Bake in an oven at gas mark 6, 400°F (200°C) for 10 minutes and then lower to gas mark 5, 375°F (190°C) for 20 minutes. Serve piping hot with a garnish of lemon.

Fillet of Lamb Orange

1 lb fillet of lamb	1 tsp arrowroot
1 tsp rosemary	½ pint stock
1 large measure Grand Marnier	1 oz butter
	1 fl oz oil
Juice of 2 oranges and grated rind of ½ orange	Salt and pepper

Gently heat the butter and oil in a sauté pan. Cut the fillets of lamb into 4-inch pieces and quickly brown all over in the oil and butter. Add the teaspoonful of rosemary and stir in well. Pour on the generous measure of orange liqueur, heat quickly and set alight . . . remember to watch your eyebrows! Gently blend the arrowroot with the orange juice, add to the pan with the stock and season to taste. Grate in the rind of half of one of the oranges. Place in a casserole and put in the oven at gas mark 4, 350°F (180°C), for about 30 minutes. The aroma when the lid is lifted is superb.

Strawberry Marquise

1 lb strawberries	¾ pint double cream
1 pineapple	1 egg white
1 level tbsp caster sugar	1 oz caster sugar
1 measure Kirsch	

Wash and hull the strawberries and cut them in half. Cut the pineapple in half, remove the woody core and purée the flesh from one half. Cut the other half into small cubes. Mix the hulled strawberries and the pineapple cubes and pour over the measure of Kirsch. Sprinkle the tablespoon of caster sugar on the top and allow to marinate for a couple of hours.

Lightly whip the cream and fold in the puréed pineapple. Whisk the egg white until stiff and fold in the sugar. Now gently fold together the pineapple cream and the egg white. Place most of the halved strawberries and pineapple cubes into a serving dish with the juices, keeping a few strawberries back. Top with the pineapple cream and decorate with the strawberries. Allow to chill before serving.

DINNER PARTY
MENU 11

Oyster Stew
Rare Cold Beef
Strawberries Escoffier

Peter Nicolls is a friend from Carlisle days. A former hotel inspector for the RAC, his delight in good food is obvious. He discovered this recipe for Oyster Stew in a book about Chesapeake Bay in the 1880s. I have adapted it and found that it works.

Rare Cold Beef is not enjoyed by everyone, but I and many of my friends love it. The way of cooking it is provided once again by Bunty Capel. It must be chilled well and served thinly cut so that the flavour of the beef really comes through.

Strawberries Escoffier makes a classic end to this menu. It is best served in a dish which is itself standing in a dish full of ice.

Oyster Stew

48 oysters	2 oz butter
6 oz smoked streaky bacon	2 tbsp vegetable oil
8 medium-sized onions	$\frac{1}{2}$ pint milk
2 stalks celery	5 fl oz single cream
1 tbsp cornflour	

Gently fry the diced bacon until it is really crisp. Remove the bacon. Chop the onions finely, add them to the pan with the butter and soften but do not brown them. Add the finely chopped celery as well. Cook until softened. Open all the oysters over the pan, off the heat, and catch all their juices. Cook the oysters for about 5 minutes, browning them on each side. Blend the cornflour with a little of the milk before pouring on the rest of it. Add to the pan, stirring the mixture over a gentle heat until the sauce begins to thicken. Allow to simmer for about 5 minutes. Take off the heat and add the single cream. Pour into heated bowls and garnish with the hot crisp bacon.

Rare Cold Beef

3–4 lb topside   1 piece beef dripping

Set the oven at gas mark 6, 400°F (200°C).

A cast-iron frying pan is best for this. Put on a high heat and get it *red-hot*, or almost! Sear the joint on all sides, taking care to seal the corners as well. This is very important.

Place the joint on a baking dish, lay the piece of dripping on the top and roast in the oven at gas mark 6, 400°F (200°C) for not a second longer than 45 minutes.

Allow the joint to cool and then wrap in foil or cling film and chill overnight in a very cold refrigerator – but be careful not to let it become frostbitten!

Slice the meat very thinly with a very sharp carving knife.

Strawberries Escoffier

1½ lb strawberries   A generous measure
½ lb clear honey   orange liqueur
½ pint water   1 large orange

Clean and hull the strawberries and cut them in half. Place them in a shallow serving dish. Gently heat the water and honey in a thick pan and gently simmer for a few minutes. Allow the syrup to cool and mix in the liqueur. Pour over the strawberries, cover with cling film and allow to chill in a refrigerator. Squeeze on the juice of the orange and finely grate the rind on top.

DINNER PARTY
MENU 12

Crab Mousse
Pheasant Breasts in a Port Wine Sauce
Poire William Sorbet

This Crab Mousse is a useful way of making a little go a long way. You'll find it's a delicious and tasty treat.

The first pheasants that I ever had were in Suffolk when we were always presented with a brace or two during the season. However you acquire yours, whether shot or otherwise killed, please make sure that they are hung for a few days . . . I like mine hung ten days, but this is too strong for many people's taste.

After such rich food I suggest this pear sorbet. I picked up the recipe in the South of France, and if there is one dish that I would like to have as the final word it is this one. . . .

Happy cooking.

Crab Mousse

1 lb crabmeat
A sachet of gelatine
3 tbsp cold water
4 fl oz mayonnaise
2 limes
2 lemons
1 oz coarsely chopped
  parsley
1 oz coarsely chopped
  chives
1 tbsp Dijon mustard
A pinch of mace
5 fl oz soured cream
3 egg whites
Salt and black pepper
1 oz butter

Dissolve the gelatine as instructed with the water, and gently blend with the mayonnaise (it should be at room temperature or above). Whisk in the juice of the lemons and limes and then fold in the parsley and chives. Add the mustard, mace and soured cream. Now fold in the crabmeat. Whisk the egg whites until stiff. Fold into the mixture and adjust the seasoning. Do not make it too smooth. Butter a mould or dish – you can find large crab-shaped moulds which are rather fun. Turn the mixture into the mould and chill well until set.

Pheasant Breasts in a Port Wine Sauce

1 pheasant breast per person	1 wineglass game stock
1 oz plain flour	6 oz chopped mushrooms
2 oz thyme-flavoured butter	1 lemon
1 wineglass port	1 oz butter
	Seasoning

The problem with using just the pheasant breasts is to know what to do with the rest of the birds! We solved that one earlier (see the Game Pâté on p.16). Make sure the breasts, or suprêmes if you would like the posh name, are skinned and cleaned. Roll them in the plain flour and put on one side. Now blend together 2 oz butter and about a teaspoonful of thyme (dried will do). Add to this any left-over flour.

Gently heat the butter in a thick pan and add the pheasant breasts, turning them gently until almost cooked. Remove, and place in a warm oven covered with foil. Turn the heat up under the pan and add the port, rapidly bringing it to the boil before setting light to it to flambé the juices. Now add the stock and gently simmer for a few minutes to reduce the sauce.

In the meantime finely chop the mushrooms and marinate them in the juice of the lemon. Grate the rind of half the lemon finely into the sauce and then add the mushrooms in the juice and cook for 1 minute more. Pour the sauce over the pheasant breasts after adjusting the seasoning, adding a little butter to give the sauce a nice glaze.

Poire William Sorbet

1 lb ripe William pears
8 oz caster sugar
½ pint water

A generous measure pear liqueur

Make a syrup of the water and sugar by boiling together until the sugar is completely dissolved.

Peel the pears and liquidise them or put them through a food processor until you have a fine purée. Mix this into the cooled syrup and add the alcohol.

Freeze for 40 minutes and then beat with a wooden spoon or silver fork. Then freeze again.